Communication

Deborah Cannarella

Jane Fournier

The Rourke Press
Vero Beach, Florida

Photo credits

All photos © copyright: AP/Wide World Photos, p. 18 top; Argonne National Laboratory, pp. 26–27 and 31; Cameramann Int'l., Ltd., pp. 23 top, 25 top; The Computer Museum History Center, p. 22 top and bottom; Corbis, pp. 4 bottom and 9 top; Corbis/Baldwin H. Ward, pp. 10 top, 18 bottom; Corbis-Bettmann, pp. 8 bottom, 12 top, 13 top, 14 top, 15 top, 17 top and bottom, 20 middle and bottom; Corbis-Reuters, p. 30 bottom; Hewlett Packard, pp. 27 middle and 29 bottom; John Springer/Corbis-Bettmann, p. 16 bottom; Marty Katz, pp. 27 bottom and 28 bottom; Mitsubishi, p. 29 top; Motorola Corp., pp. 1 and 24 top; North Wind Picture Archives, pp. 6 bottom, 10 bottom, 11 bottom; PhotoDisc, pp. 24 bottom, 27 top and 28 top; PhotoEdit, pp. 23 bottom, 25 bottom; Sony Corp., p. 22 middle; Space Center, p. 21 top (Ron Keller, photographer); Stock Montage, Inc., pp. 6 top, 4 top and 7 top (Newberry Library), 4–5 and 7 bottom, 8 top, 9 bottom, 4 middle and 11 top, 12 bottom, 13 bottom, 14 bottom; Unicorn Stock Photos, p. 15 bottom (Jerry Barner); UPI/Corbis-Bettmann, pp. 16 top, 19, 20 top, 21 bottom. Page 30 top: SoftBook® image used courtesy of SoftBook® Press, Inc. www.softbook.com, SoftBook® is a registered trademark of SoftBook® Press, Inc. All cover and introduction page images PhotoDisc.

An Editorial Directions Book
Book design and production by Criscola Design

Library of Congress Cataloging-in-Publication Data

Cannarella, Deborah.
    Communications / Deborah Cannarella, Jane Fournier.
    p. cm. — (Into the next millennium)
    Includes index.
    Summary : Text and photographs present a brief overview of the history of communications from cuneiform writing in the first century B.C. to the Internet and videoconferencing at the end of the twentieth century.
    ISBN 1-57103-271-1
    1. Communication—History Juvenile literature. [1. Communciation History.] I. Fournier, Jane, 1955–   . II. Title. III. Series.
    P91.2.C28 1999
    302.2'09—dc21   99-27205
                                                           CIP

Introduction

The history of the human race is a story of great discoveries and amazing achievements. Since ancient times, people have found creative solutions to problems, met impossible challenges, and turned visions into reality. Each of these remarkable people—and each of their contributions—changed the world they lived in forever. Together, they created the world we know and live in today.

The six books in this series—*Medicine, Transportation, Communication, Exploration, Engineering,* and *Sports*—present a timeline of the great discoveries and inventions that have shaped our world. As you travel from ancient to modern times, you will discover the many ways in which people have worked to heal sickness, shape materials, share information, explore strange places, and achieve new goals. Although they worked with many different tools, their goal was always the same: to improve our quality of life.

As we enter the twenty-first century, we will continue to build on what each generation of people before us has created and discovered. With the knowledge they have given us, we will discover new ways to build, heal, communicate, discover, and achieve. We will continue to change the world in ways we can only begin to imagine.

From the *Past...*

5000 B.C.

Ancient peoples developed systems of writing that used pictures and symbols—instead of alphabets—to represent objects and numbers. One of the earliest writing systems is **cuneiform.** Symbols shaped like wedges or triangles were cut into clay, metal, or stone with a tool called a stylus. Cuneiform was the basis of many languages until about the first century B.C.

The first writing inks were used in ancient Egypt and China in about 2500 B.C. Some early inks were made from natural red, blue, and black materials—such as berries, indigo, tree bark, and soot.

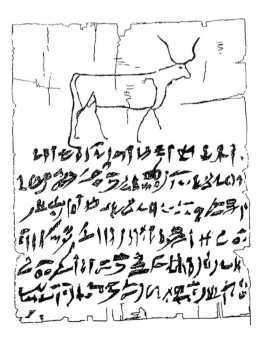

2700 B.C.

The ancient Egyptians used the fibers of the plant called papyrus to make a type of **paper.** Strips of the plant were pressed together and dried in the sun to form a pure white paper. The sheets were then joined together to make long scrolls (rolls). The Egyptians—and later the Greeks and Romans—used the paper, which was also called papyrus, to make books and letters.

500

During the Middle Ages, monks in monasteries wrote and decorated books by hand. These books were called **illuminated manuscripts.** The word *illuminated* refers to the bright colors and the precious metals—such as gold—used to decorate the pages. Most of the illuminated manuscripts were Bibles, prayer books, hymn books, and books of poetry.

The first known printed book was made in China in 868. Each page was carved out of a block of wood. Ink was spread on the carving and transferred to a piece of paper. This process is known as block printing. The pages were bound together to make the book.

1440

Johannes Gutenberg invented the **printing press** in about 1440. In his system, called movable type, each letter of the alphabet was made out of a piece of metal. In 1456, Gutenberg printed a copy of the Bible in Latin. He and his assistants printed 150 copies. By 1500, there were more than 1,000 print shops in Europe, and millions of books had been printed.

1500

The first camera was the **camera obscura.** The name means "dark chamber." This camera was a large box with a tiny hole in one side. When light passed through the hole, an upside-down image of the scene outside formed on the inside wall of the box. Artists often used the camera obscura for their drawings. They could sit inside the box and trace and color the images that appeared on the wall.

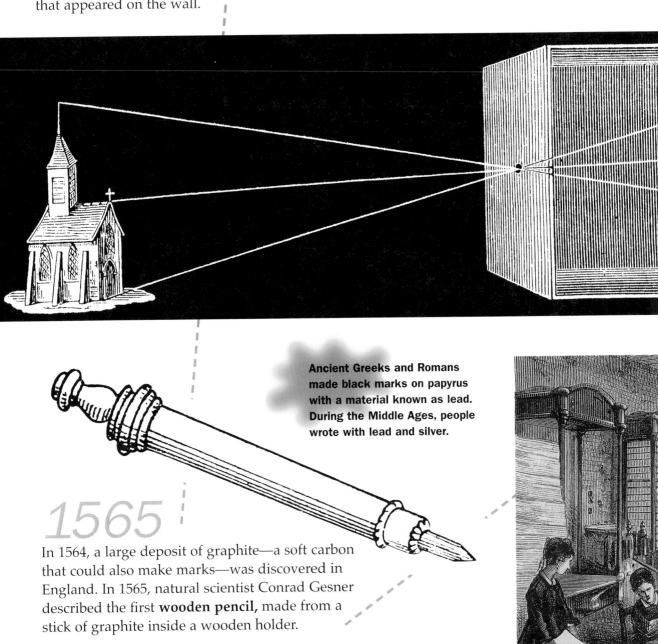

Ancient Greeks and Romans made black marks on papyrus with a material known as lead. During the Middle Ages, people wrote with lead and silver.

1565

In 1564, a large deposit of graphite—a soft carbon that could also make marks—was discovered in England. In 1565, natural scientist Conrad Gesner described the first **wooden pencil,** made from a stick of graphite inside a wooden holder.

1796

Alois Senefelder invented a printing process known as **lithography.** He drew images on the surface of a smooth stone with special inks. He made several copies of a design by pressing sheets of paper against the inked stone. By 1850, the first lithographic press—a machine with rollers to spread the ink—was operating. Today, lithography is an important part of the printing of books, magazines, and newspapers.

In 1814, the London newspaper *The Times* was the first to use a steam-powered press to print large numbers of copies hundreds of times faster than ever before.

1810

By 1810, there were about 185 **paper mills** in the United States. Before the invention of the paper machine in 1798, paper was made one sheet at a time. A screen was dipped into a tub that contained water and the paper material— usually linen, cotton, or ground wood pulp. After the mold was lifted out of the water, the material on the screen was pressed and dried into sheets.

1827

Louis Daguerre (right) created the first successful process of **photography.** He treated a thin sheet of silver-coated copper to make the metals sensitive to light. Then he placed the sheet inside his camera and exposed it to light. When the sheet was later treated with chemicals, the areas that had been exposed to light revealed an image. These early photographs were called daguerreotypes.

The first telephone company was the Bell Telephone Company, formed by Alexander Graham Bell, Thomas Watson, and two other partners in 1877.

w   h   a   t

h   a   t   h

G   0   D

w   r   0   u

g   h   t. ?

1837

A **telegraph** is a device for sending messages through wires by electricity. In 1837, Samuel Morse created a simple machine that ran on batteries. The Morse telegraph sent messages using a code of dots and dashes to represent letters. This system of symbols is known as Morse code.

1868

Newspaper editor Christopher Latham Sholes and two partners were the first to develop the practical **typewriter.** E. Remington and Sons bought their idea and sold the first typewriters in 1874. Early keyboards were arranged alphabetically, and the typewriters could type only capital letters. The first shift-key typewriter—the Remington Model 2—was sold in 1878.

The first telephone exchange opened in New Haven, Connecticut, in 1878. It had 21 customers, who placed their calls through an operator.

Although it was never built, the first fax (facsimile) machine was invented in 1843 by Alexander Bain, a mechanic from Scotland. In 1851, Frederick Blakewell demonstrated his electrical fax machine. The image was written on tinfoil, wrapped around a cylinder, and then transmitted.

1876

In 1876, inventor Alexander Graham Bell spoke to his assistant Thomas Watson on the first **telephone.** The first message was, "Mr. Watson, come here. I want you!" Bell's telephone was the first device to send speech sounds across electric wires.

1877

As entertainment, painted or photographic glass slides were displayed in a **magic lantern,** an early type of projector. The slides were shown one at a time, but if they were moved quickly, it would seem as if the images were moving on the screen.

Eadweard Muybridge was the first to capture live action on film. He set up **12** cameras to photograph a running horse at different stages of motion. Muybridge mounted the images on a rotating disk and projected them onto a screen to produce a "moving" picture of the horse galloping.

The first phonograph recording was of Thomas Edison reciting the verse "Mary Had a Little Lamb."

1877

A phonograph is a device that plays recorded sounds. The first practical **phonograph** was invented by Thomas Alva Edison. As a person spoke through the mouthpiece, the vibrations of the sound were recorded on tinfoil wrapped around a metal cylinder. The sounds could then be played back with a needle that traced the impressions on the tinfoil.

ESTERBROOK'S STEEL PENS.

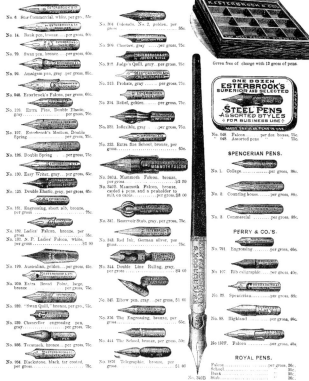

READ THE PREFACE BEFORE ORDERING.

1884

Thick reeds, brushes, and quill pens made from bird feathers were the earliest types of writing instruments. In 1828, John Mitchell made the first machine-made pen points, called nibs. Pens with steel nibs had to be dipped into ink before they could write. In 1884, L. E. Waterman invented the first **fountain pen.** This pen held its own ink and did not need to be dipped.

1887

Emil Berliner improved Edison's phonograph by recording sounds on a flat disk instead of on a cylinder. These disks, known as records, were played on a machine called a gramophone. The Victor Talking Machine Company created its own **record player** called the Victrola.

John H. Loud, an American inventor, patented the first ballpoint pen in 1888. A ballpoint pen has a metal ball at its tip, which rolls ink onto a writing surface as it rotates.

Victor

Victor V
$60

Other Styles
$10 to $300

You owe it to yourself to hear the Victor. The very next time you pass a Victor dealer's, stop in—he will gladly play any Victor music you wish to hear. Write for catalogues.

1888

George Eastman made the first **camera** for the general public. This lightweight camera (right) contained a roll of paper-based film. After taking the pictures, photographers sent the camera to the Eastman Company. Eastman sent back prints and the camera, with a new roll of film inside. By 1900, Eastman made the Brownie, a camera with a removable container of transparent, plastic film. It was intended for use by children.

In 1892, Thomas Edison and his assistant, W. K. L. Dickson, invented the kinetoscope, the first motion-picture device that used a roll of film. The machine had a peephole or eyepiece on top, so only one person could watch the film at a time.

1895

Inspired by Thomas Edison's kinetoscope, the brothers Louis and Auguste Lumière created the first combination motion-picture camera, printer, and projector. Their invention was called the cinématographe. The brothers made more than 40 **motion pictures** in 1896—most of them about everyday life in France.

In 1896, the first dial telephones went into use in Milwaukee, Wisconsin.

1906

The first **radio program** in the United States was broadcast to offshore ships by Reginald Fessenden on Christmas Eve 1906. The first commercial radio stations were KDKA in Philadelphia—which broadcast the 1920 presidential election—and WWJ in Detroit. By the end of 1921, there were eight commercial stations in the United States. Radio was a major source of entertainment until the 1950s, when television became popular.

In 1895, Guglielmo Marconi invented the wireless telegraph, or radio. A radio sends signals through the air instead of through electric wires. The "wireless" was first used for ship-to-ship and ship-to-shore communication. Radio helped save many victims of sea disasters—including the survivors of the *Titanic* sinking in 1912.

1926

John L. Baird invented the first **television**—a device that transmits moving pictures by changing light and sound waves into electricity. He broadcast pictures from London to New York. In 1928, Vladimir Zworykin—who made improvements on Baird's television—developed the first color television system.

1927

New York City and San Francisco were connected by the first transcontinental phone call in 1915. The first **transatlantic telephone service**—between New York City and London—began in 1927.

The movie, *The Jazz Singer,* made in 1927, was the first **"talkie"**—a motion picture with dialogue. *The Jazz Singer* was actually a silent film with singing and speech added to it—but its success ended the era of the silent movie. By the 1930s, the film's producer, Warner Brothers, was making about 100 "talking" motion pictures a year.

1936

Isaac Shoenberg created a **television-broadcast system,** which was launched in London in 1936. In 1939, the National Broadcasting Company (NBC) announced it would begin broadcasting for two hours a week. By the mid-1940s, there were 23 television stations in the United States.

The Federal Communications Commission (FCC) was created in 1934. This agency of the government supervises communication made by radio, wire, and cable. It also regulates radio and television stations.

1937

The process of **xerography** was developed in 1937 by Chester F. Carlson. Xerography is an electrical method of producing exact copies of written and printed material. The Haloid Company, which later changed its name to the Xerox Corporation, bought Carlson's idea. The company sold the first xerographic copy machine in 1960.

1945

The first electronic digital computer was built by John Atanasoff in 1939. The first general-purpose electronic digital computer, known as **ENIAC,** was built in 1945. ENIAC (Electronic Numerical Integrator and Computer) had the same electrical circuitry (plan) as modern high-speed computers. It operated with vacuum tubes—which were also used for radio broadcasting, long-distance telephone service, and television.

ENIAC was about 8 feet (2.5 m) high and 79 feet (24 m) long and weighed more than 30 tons. It could calculate about 5,000 addition problems and 1,000 multiplication problems per second—more than 1,000 times faster than other computers at that time.

1948

Columbia Records was the first to develop **long-playing records,** or LPs. These records were made of unbreakable plastic and rotated at the speed of 33.3 revolutions per minute (rpm). They played up to 30 minutes of sound on each side. The smaller, 45-rpm record, called a single, held 8 minutes of sound per side. Earlier records played at the speed of 78 rpm for about 4.5 minutes per side.

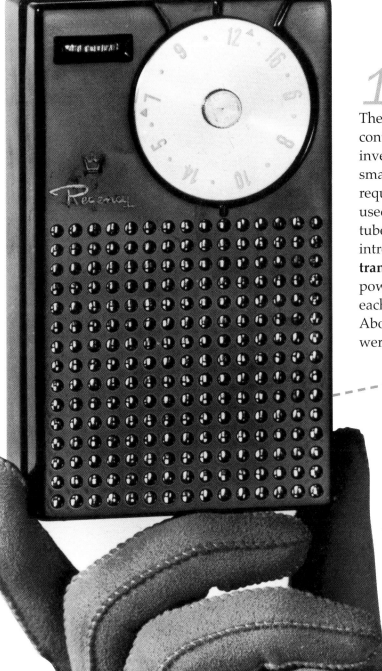

1954

The transistor, a small device that controls electric currents, was invented in 1947. Because it was smaller, more reliable, and required less power, it was often used in place of the vacuum tube. In 1954, Texas Instruments introduced the first pocket-sized **transistor radio.** The battery that powered the four transistors in each radio lasted for 20 hours. About 1,500 transistor radios were sold the first year.

In 1900, Valdemar Poulsen made a magnetic recording of human speech on steel wire. Scientists developed the magnetic tape recorder during World War II (1939–1945). By 1950, magnetic tape was being used instead of phonograph records for radio programs and for recording.

1962

Echo 1, the first **communications satellite,** was launched into Earth's orbit in 1960. The satellite was able to receive radio signals and reflect them back to Earth. The satellite *Telstar* (left) was launched in 1962. It was the first satellite able to receive signals from one station on Earth and send them to another. Telstar sent the first television pictures across the Atlantic Ocean—from Maine to England and France.

In 1956, Charles P. Ginsburg and Ray Dolby of Ampex Corporation developed the first videotape recorder.

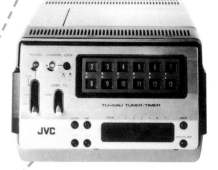

1969

The first **videocassette recorders** (VCR) were introduced in 1969. A VCR is a device that records and plays films, home movies, and television programs on magnetic tape.

1970

The first **IMAX film** was shown at the World's Fair in Japan in 1970. An IMAX screen or dome is more than eight stories high. Each frame of IMAX film is 10 times larger than each frame of the film shown in regular movie theaters. Multiple speakers deliver clear sound to every section of the theater. The first IMAX 3-D (three-dimensional) film was shown in Canada in 1986.

By the early 1980s, small videocassette recorders were combined with video cameras in one unit called a camcorder. These portable devices are powered by batteries. The videotapes can be viewed on a television and, unlike film, can be erased and re-recorded.

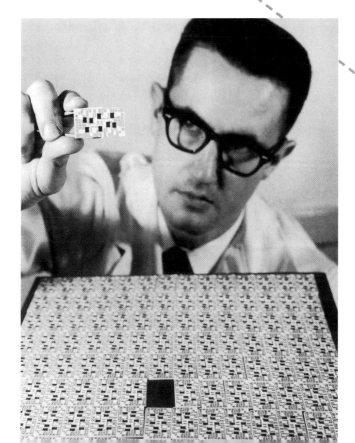

1971

The **microprocessor** is a small, electronic chip that contain hundreds of thousands—even millions—of transistor circuits. The first microprocessors were made for desktop calculators in 1971. These chips made it possible to build much smaller computers than ever before. Today, microprocessors control personal computers, video games, digital watches, microwave ovens, and other household appliances.

1974

The first **personal computer** (PC) for sale to the general public was the Altair 8800. This machine was sold as a kit. Buyers had to put the computer together themselves. There was no keyboard or video display terminal. To enter information, the user had to set switches on the front of the machine.

In 1975, William Gates and Paul Allen wrote BASIC, the first programming language for a personal computer. They later founded the company Microsoft. The name was a shortened form of the words *microcomputer* and *software*. Software refers to the programs that a computer uses to perform tasks.

1981

In 1981, the Japanese company Sony created the first **Walkman**—a portable radio and cassette player. The company has continued to develop miniature, portable, and wearable sound and image technology—including videocassette recorders and players, personal televisions, and digital audiotape stereos.

Pocket, or palm-sized, computers are so small and lightweight that they can be carried in a pocket, briefcase, or purse.

The first **portable computer** was the Osborne 1, developed by Adam Osborne in 1981. The machine weighed 4.5 pounds (10 kg), and the screen was 5 inches (12.7 cm) across the diagonal. The same year, Epson introduced the HX-20, the first notebook, or book-sized, computer.

1982

In 1977, Steven P. Jobs and Stephen G. Wozniak introduced the **first, pre-built computer**—the Apple II. International Business Machines (IBM) introduced its first personal computer in 1981. Early computers—like this Commodore 64 introduced in 1982—used television screens instead of computer monitors.

In 1975, there was one computer for every 1,000 people in the United States. Ten years after the introduction of the PC, there were 90 computers for every 1,000 people.

A CD can store millions of pieces of information—including text, sound, still pictures, and moving images. The *Electronic Encyclopedia*, created in 1986, was the first CD-ROM Encyclopedia. It contained the text of the *Academic American Encyclopedia*.

Compact discs, or CDs, are aluminum and plastic discs that store sound and information. To record a CD, sound waves are translated into electric signals. The signals are stored on the disc as a numerical code. A laser beam reads the code and translates the electric signals back into sound. A CD-ROM (Compact Disc Read Only Memory) can store information, pictures, and sound—as well as video games and computer software.

1983

Cellular phones are portable telephones that combine radio, telephone, and computer technology. Some types of cellular phones are mounted in automobiles and powered by the car's engine. Other types, small enough to carry in the owner's hand or pocket, are powered by batteries. The FCC first licensed commercial cellular-phone systems in 1983.

Digital cameras do not record an image on film. Instead, they convert color and light into digital information. The images can then be viewed on a television screen or computer. The first digital cameras for use by the general public were presented in 1994.

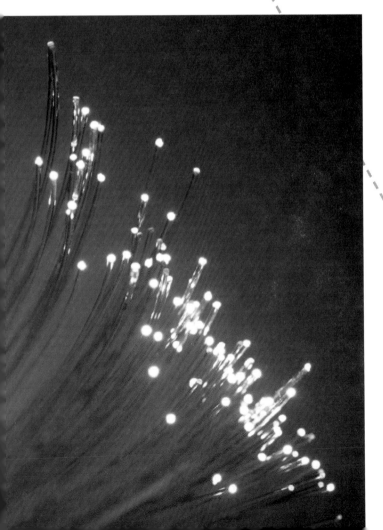

1988

Cables made of optical fibers first carried telephone messages across the Atlantic Ocean in 1988. In a **fiber-optic cable,** sound signals travel across the thin strands of plastic or glass as light. Fiber-optic cables can carry thousands of times more information than other types of cables.

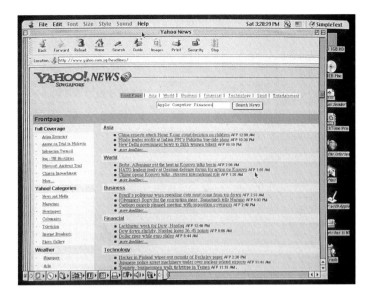

1992

The **Internet** is a huge network of small, linked computer networks that contain many types of information. The World Wide Web (WWW), also known as the Web, provides links to this information through electronic documents, called pages. People use a browser, such as Netscape, to view the pages. Search engines, such as Yahoo, allow people to find the pages that contain the information they want. The Internet also makes it possible for people to communicate electronically through discussion groups and e-mail.

A DVD (Digital Video Disc) is a type of compact disc developed in 1997. It allows videos to be stored digitally on disc, rather than magnetically on tape. DVDs are considered the first multimedia disc because they can store information, sound, and motion pictures.

1995

The introduction of **Windows 95,** "user-friendly" software from Microsoft, together with improved computer designs— such as powerful, lightweight notebooks—have led to the widespread use of personal computers. By 1997, there were about 117 million computers in use in the United States. More than 95 percent were personal computers.

...Into the *Future*

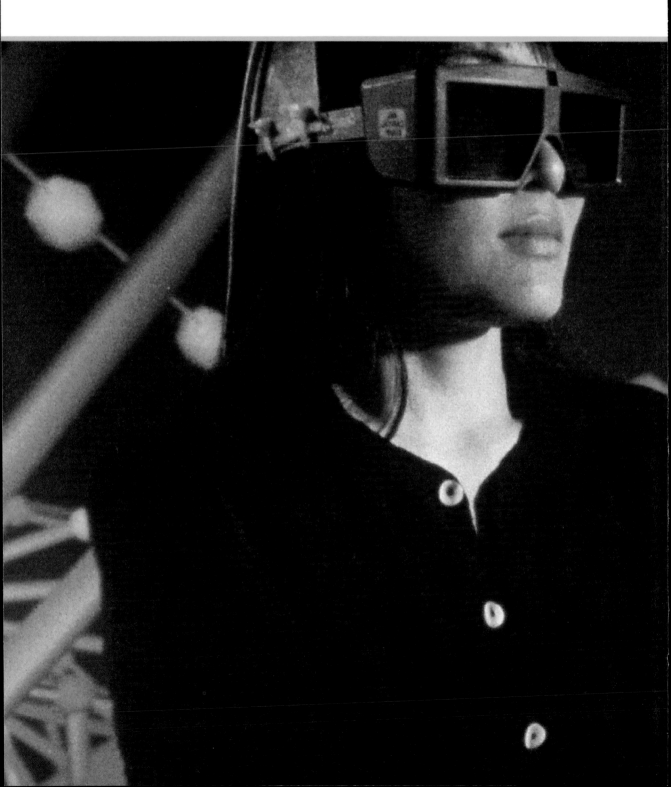

Satellite telephones.
Cellular phones depend on ground-based relay stations, so their calling range is limited. Satellite phones relay signals to and from a group of satellites that orbit Earth at a low altitude (about 500 miles or 800 km). These satellites can direct signals to and from any part of Earth's surface.

Engineers expect to produce battery-powered wrist phones that are close in size to a wristwatch. The wearer will activate the phone by voice and by simple one- or two-button commands.

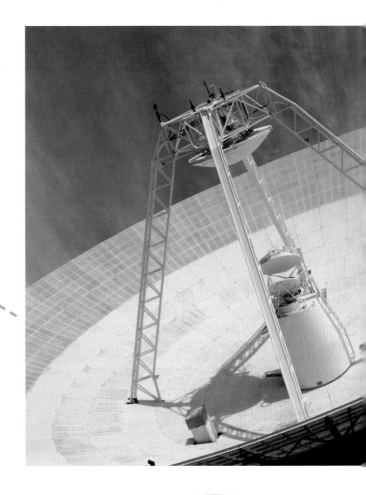

Wearable PCs.
Engineers are designing small wearable computers that will allow people to have constant, easy access to computer services. These PCs may be the size of wristwatches or portable CD players. Some may look like eye-glasses with monitors built into the lenses. Most of these wearable computers will be too small to have a keyboard, so instead will be controlled by voice.

High-definition TV.
High-definition television (HDTV) projects digital pictures that have a density of 720 or 1080 lines. Standard television signals, which are read as waves, project pictures with a density of only 525 lines. The higher resolution of HDTV will create sharper, clearer pictures. Its sound system, called surround sound, will also deliver clearer sound. HDTV can also be used to display digital computer information, such as web pages and e-mail.

Customized CDs.
Instead of buying CDs from a store, music lovers will soon download music from the Internet. They will select individual songs and artists from samples, then pay for and download the music electronically. With special computer software, users will be able to listen to the music and make a CD of the selections with a recordable CD drive (CD-R).

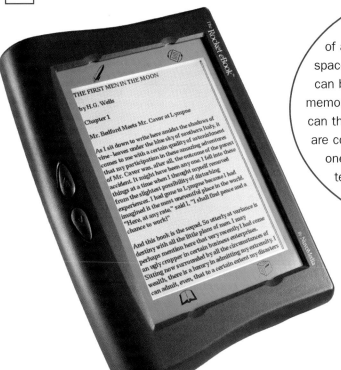

E-books.
An electronic book, or e-book, consists of a flat screen, a small computer, and storage space called memory. Electronic text in digital form can be purchased and downloaded to the e-book's memory through the Internet or a phone line. The text can then be read on the screen at any time. E-books are compact and reusable and can store more than one book at a time. E-books may soon replace textbooks and other types of printed books that need to have their information updated often.

Soon, people will have customized Internet newspapers—containing just the news stories that interest them—delivered daily to their personal computers. Engineers are even developing reusable and flexible computer screens. Internet readers will be able to download their morning "paper," roll it up, and carry it with them to read later in the day.

Virtual-reality headsets. Virtual-reality technology projects 3-D images created by computers. The viewer wears a special headset and sensors. With this technology—and the help of robots—scientists and engineers will explore dangerous or distant places. They will even be able to explore places that are physically impossible to reach—such as inside a molecule—as if they were actually there. Virtual-reality technology will have many uses, including education and entertainment.

Plasma display panels. Engineers are working to develop thin video screens—called plasma display panels—for computers, televisions, and phones. Tiny pockets of gas are sandwiched between two sheets of glass. The gas molecules react with chemicals to produce red, green, or blue light. The displays deliver large, high-quality, color images on a screen that is less than 6 inches (15.2 cm) thick.

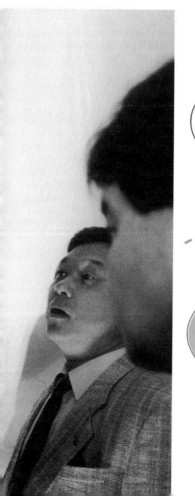

The Internet and videoconferencing (meeting through video) will expand education opportunities in remote locations. Students will attend classes on the Internet. Teachers and students will interact through e-mail, Internet chat rooms, and by phone. Completed assignments will be turned in and, after being graded, returned by e-mail. Experts anywhere in the world can "visit" classrooms through long-distance video connections.

Index

Ballpoint pens, 13
Bell, Alexander Graham, 10, 11
Books, printed, 7
Camcorders, 21
Cameras
    Digital, 24
    and George Eastman, 14
    Obscura, 8
CD-ROMs, 23
Cellular phones, 24
Communications satellites, 20
Compact discs, 23, 29
Computers
    First electronic digital, 18
    Personal, 22, 23
    Pocket, 23
    Portable, 22
    Wearable, 28
Cuneiform, 6
Digital Video Discs (DVD), 25
Distance learning, 31
Edison, Thomas, 12, 14
Electronic Numerical Integrator
    and Computer (ENIAC), 18
E-books, 30
E-mail, 23
Fax (facsimile) machines, 11

Fiber-optic cables, 24
Fountain pens, 13
High-definition TV, 29
Illuminated manuscripts, 7
IMAX, 21
Internet, 25, 30, 31
Kinetoscope, 14
Lead, 8
Lithography, 9
Magic lantern, 12
Magnetic tape recorders, 19
Microprocessors, 21
Microsoft, 22, 25
Morse, Samuel, 10
Motion pictures, 12, 14, 16
Paper, 6
Paper mills, 9
Papyrus, 6, 8
Phonographs, 12, 19
Photographic process, 10
Plasma display panels, 31
Presses
    Printing, 7
    Steam-powered, 9
Radio
    Programs, 15, 19
    Transistor, 19

Record players, 13
Records, long-playing, 18
Satellite telephones, 28
"Talkies," 16
Telegraph, 10
Telephones, 11, 14
Televisions, 15
Television-broadcast system, 17
Transatlantic telephone service,
    16
Typewriter, 11
Videocassette recorders, 20,
    21
Videoconferencing, 31
Videotape recorders, 20
Virtual reality headsets, 31
Walkmans, 22
Windows 95, 25
Wooden pencils, 8
Wrist phones, 28
Xerography, 17

For further reading

Books

Davidson, Margaret. Illustrations by Stephen Marchesi. *The Story of Alexander Graham Bell: Inventor of the Telephone.* Famous Lives series. Milwaukee, WI: Gareth Stevens, 1997.

Ganeri, Anita. *The Story of Communications.* Signs of the Times series. New York: Oxford University Press, 1998.

Jay, Michael. *The History of Communication.* Science Discovery series. New York: Thomson Learning, 1995.

Skurzynski, Gloria. *Get the Message: Telecommunications in Your High-Tech World.* New York: Simon & Schuster Books for Young Readers, 1993.

Web sites

Museum of Broadcast Communications

Information on the history of radio, television, and television programs
http://www.mbcnet.org

National Aeronautics and Space Association

Information on present and future space communications
http://nasa.gov